the Lowcountry Child

Written by Monica Simmons MEd.
Photography by Wilson Baker

This book is dedicated to my grandmother, Helen Votino. In hopes that all your days will be

days in the Lowcountry.

TODAY'S KIDS PUBLISHERS
© August 1995

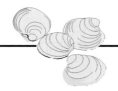

My name is Bo. I live in the South Carolina Lowcountry. I live right along the

 marsh. I swim in the river that runs through the MARSH. The

oak trees live in the marsh, too. They are good for climbing, so I usually do.

I have a dog named Bubba 2. His name is Bubba 2 because Bubba 1 ran away.

When he ran away, we never saw him again, I guess he just kept running.

Then I got a new puppy. I wanted to remember Bubba 1, so I named the new

puppy Bubba 2. Bubba 2 is a good dog.

He likes to swim. In the

Lowcountry, there is lots of water

to swim in. Bubba 2 is a water dog, so

he has webbed feet. If he sees a marsh or a river or

a pond, he jumps right in and gets wet.

He bites at the fish and the crabs that he can see with his

razor sharp vision. So, he is the perfect dog for

me. I am always around the ocean, or the fishing

boats, because that is what the LOWCOUNTRY is,

it is the marshland along the coast of South Carolina.

Life in the Lowcountry is full of fishing and
crabbing and swimming and shrimping and
going to the beaches. Life in the Lowcountry
is good. And, me and Bubba 2, we like the
good life.

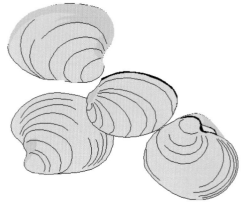

Some days Bubba 2 and me, we go with Pa Pa to the islands. On those days, we get

oysters, crabs, fish, and, sometimes, shrimp. First, we go from Hilton Head Island

to Callawassie Island. Then, we might go to Lady's Island, Beaufort, Dataw Island,

Distant Island, Hunting Island, and St. Helena's Island all in one day. These

islands are BARRIER ISLANDS. They are along the coast of

the South Carolina Lowcountry. Some of them are big and

some of them are really small. They are called BARRIER

ISLANDS because they create a barrier from the OCEAN

WINDS and CURRENTS for the mainland. Many of them have lighthouses to

warn the ships coming in from sea. On the days we go fishing and crabbing, we sell

seafood to the markets

on the bigger islands.

Some days we sell our

catch to the restaurants.

It all depends on what we

catch in our nets.

Other days, I go down to the beach with my friends. We use nets and chicken necks. We catch BLUE CRABS. Mom likes to cook blue crabs, so I take them home to boil. Once in a while, I pick oysters along the intra-coastal waterway with a friend of mine who is a fisherman.

8

I can't go up that far by myself, so I wait until

Captain Jones has some free time. Then we take a

BATEAU and go out in the FLAT-

LANDS. The bateau is a special boat, built for col-

lecting oysters. A bateau has a plank bottom.

9

We get clusters of oysters with GRABS. Grabs are special metal tongs made by

local welders. SINGLES, or oysters that are not in clusters, are collected with

metal tongs set on long, stout handles. We use eight to

sixteen foot tongs. We thrust them straight

down over the edge of the boat. We open and close

them to rake the bottom, then lift them hand over hand to the surface, full of

oysters. Oystering is the hardest work that we do. Shoveling oysters from a

bateau is nothing but hard work.

Other days I go out to sea with Captain Jones. Captain Jones takes me to help him when he casts his nets to fish for chum to use on his charter. We use CAST NETS. The nets are handmade in Beaufort County. The length of the net matches the height of the person casting. The size of the mesh determines what a net will catch. A wide mesh will hold mullet and shrimp. A "poor man's net" captures everything. On those days, we get MENHADEN fish which can be made into an oil and used for shark fishing. They can also be fed live to the DOLPHINS. Feeding the dolphins is my favorite use for menhaden. We have to be careful when we feed menhaden to the dolphins. If I offer them a dead one, they blow SEA WATER in my face and snort. Then they slap the water with their tails as they dive down to show me that they don't like to eat dead fish!

My MOST favorite days are when I go to CHARLESTON. That's when Bubba

2 and I get to see Joe. Joe is my best friend. He likes to fish and crab and play

pirates, like the ones that used to come along the coast of South Carolina in

the 1500s. They would steal gold from the Spanish. Joe and I know where some

of it is buried. Joe's granny has seen the pirates's ghosts many times. She tells

us where they are when she tells her stories. We have an old

treasure map that we found, but we didn't dig

up the gold, yet.

We use our TELE-

SCOPES for looking

for treasures. Then we

can see the ships coming

in. We can also look for

pirates, in case they decide to come back someday.

JOE'S grandpa has a big SHRIMPING boat with a lookout. We

can mostly spot the pirates's gold from up top. Bubba 2 likes

to be the captain, and me and Joe are the first and second mates.

Bubba 2 likes it best when he NAVIGATES the ship. After

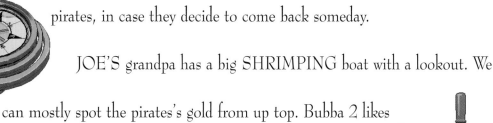

our treasure hunting, we usu-

ally find a good place to hide

the treasures that we found. We have lots of

hidden treasures in the marsh. We can look out

over the marsh if we climb up into the oak

trees. The palm trees are harder to climb, but

we can look out from them too.

Joe's granny calls us into the house along with the warm smell of HOECAKES

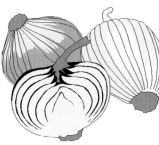

cooking in deep fat. COLLARD GREENS are in the pot. When

we eat dinner, Joe's granny sits by the fire and weaves baskets.

While she weaves, she tells of the times gone by. She tells many,

many stories by the fire. Sometimes they are the same stories and sometimes they are

not. I've been to Joe's enough times to know some of them by

heart. She tells of how her family lived and farmed in coastal

Beaufort for over three hundred years. When African and

European immigrants came to the South Carolina coast, they blended with

the American Indians. They borrowed Indian tools and techniques for farm-

ing and living off the land. I like to hear about that part because my Pa Pa is

Cherokee Indian. It seems that the lifestyle of the coast was created from the

environment. Granny makes us notice how everyone adapted to the life of

using local things to make their lives. Like how the fishermen harvest

their catch in locally made bateaus, just like

they did when she was a little girl.

Back then, seafood was caught in the rivers, creeks, and marshes. Their main food was shrimp, crabs, mullet, drumfish, oysters, and clams. She tells how the farming was mainly garden plots of corn, beans, carrots, tomatoes, onions, sugar cane, and greens.

Granny sticks by the tradition of making or growing what she needs, and making do with the resources at hand. She can make the most beautiful QUILT from remnants of cloth. It looks like a piece of art. She has drawings painted on tin. Her father made boats, nets, walking sticks, ANDIRONS, and everything else he needed. The old techniques were handed down from his grandfather. She was taught to weave baskets as a very young girl. In the older plantation system, her grandmother was a part of the slave community. From the freed workers of large rice and cotton plantations came free families who

harvested in the fields, woods, and creeks. Granny has become a preservationist simply by staying put.

Anyway, back to the hoecakes and collards. We always saved room for Granny's fruit cobbler. It was always hot and buttery and melted in your mouth. After dessert, she would sometimes tell GULLAH TALES. Other times she would tell family stories about her great grandmother's time, stories that had been passed down from generation to generation. Granny had some FOLK TALES all her own. Sometimes she would tell pirate stories. They were my favorite ones. The best is about the time her great grandmother saw pirates come to Folly Beach to bury treasures. She said that her great grandmother's name was Granny Molly. Granny Molly liked to sit out on the steps at night and chew tobacco weed that she grew in her herb garden. The night the pirates came in with three chests of gold, they buried the gold, and then they got into a fight. They were all drinking bottles of ale. She could see them staggering in the moonlight. When the shots rang out, they began to fall into the marsh near the chests that they had buried. She says the ghosts of the pirates can be heard in the marsh wandering around looking for the traitor that got away. She says she hears them crying, "MUTINY!!" through the swamp. She says it is an eerie sound, indeed.

Aside from Joe, Bubba 2 is my best friend. He's the first thing I see in the morning and the last thing I do at night is put him down. He watches out for me. He knows when a bad person is nearby. He doesn't really growl or anything, he just looks at me with that look that says, "LOOK OUT!" When he looks into my eyes like that, I know what he's thinking, and he knows I know. It's always

been like that with Bubba 2 and me. Then there's something he does that is REALLY special. He lets me know when there are ghosts around. I noticed it the first time out at Folly Beach on Halloween night.

We were all out together, there was an OYSTER ROAST and some little kids

had on costumes. Bubba 2 and me were there with my Pa Pa and

some of the fishermen. They grilled oysters and made FROG-

MORE STEW. Some of the fishermen were SHUCKING

fresh oysters and eating them raw. Bubba 2 likes oysters, but he

likes to dive for his own, and brings them up

in his teeth. Bubba 2 is a water dog. He can hold his

breath and dive in for ducks. But since we don't

really hunt much, he has learned to fish. He's pretty good at it too.

Anyway, back to Halloween night, the kids were trick or treating. One group had a beast and a Batman. One kid was a vampire. There was a little girl who was dressed all in pink. She looked like a princess. Another group, way ahead, was walking along the

road with a wagon. All of their buckets looked full of candy. They had probably been trick or treating all day. Joe's grandpa had come down from Charleston by boat. It was the one night of the year that I got to see Joe without going into Charleston. It's been a tradition for the Lowcountry fishermen to gather together off Folly Beach and enjoy the ending of the fishing and tourist season. Winter would mean boat repairs, net mending, boat railing, and overhauling motors that needed to be tended during the season when there was no time. Since the season dictated everyone's lifestyle, the Halloween gathering was a way to regroup for the coming year and compare stories. The fishermen get very little free time to exchange tales and relax, until the weather says that they can.

Back to the ghost that Bubba 2 saw, Joe and me were out in the marsh. We could see the lights from the OYSTER ROAST. We could hear the laughter in the marsh breeze, a little distant, too far away to hear the stories that were being told. There was a light in the distance. It looked like a large shrimper on the horizon of the ocean in the darkness.

We could also see the Morris Island lighthouse. It doesn't get used much anymore, so it looks kind of lonely, not lit up and all. Suddenly, Bubba 2 disappeared into the marsh. He liked to run after birds. Joe had been whittling a walking stick by the light of a kerosene lantern. We were talking about things, when Bubba 2 let out a yelp. By the sound of the yelp, Bubba 2 had gone a far piece. The intensity of the yelp got my attention. Now Bubba 2 is a brave dog, he doesn't just go around yelping like some dogs. Joe knew that, and I knew that. We looked at each other in the eyes, as we eased up together and headed in the direction of the yelp.

Joe held the lantern up to light the way. We walked through the underbrush. It was marshy and we could hear the clicking of FIDDLER CRABS as we stepped into their homes. They would scurry ahead of us, into their holes to avoid our deadly footsteps. Somewhere across the night a loon was singing a sad lament. All of that together had a real spooky feeling. Not to mention, it was Halloween and all. It can still make goosebumps when I think about it. Anyway, we called to Bubba 2 and never heard another sound, so we kept walking in the direction of the yelp. All the while, we were going deeper and deeper into the swamp.

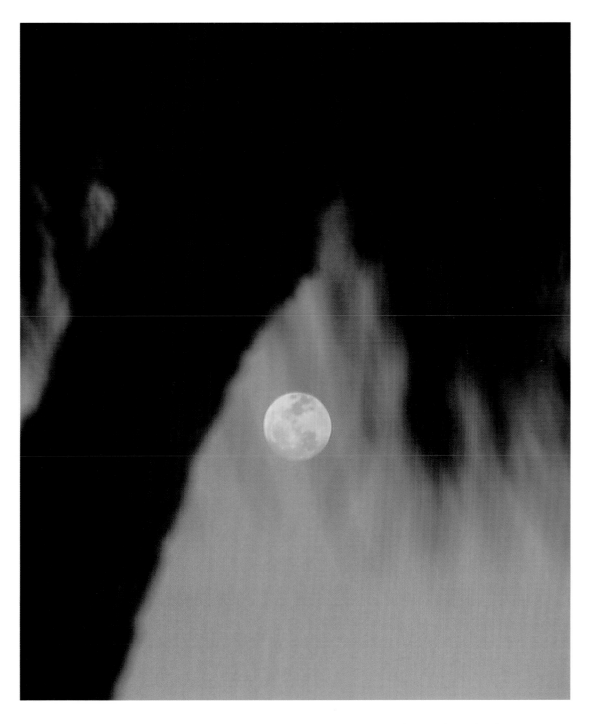

The LIVE OAK TREES began to block out the moonlight as their limbs grew in

close to each other. The SPANISH MOSS was thick on the branches and as we

looked up, we noticed that not only was the moon full, but it was bright orange.

Joe stopped to listen and he looked at me from under the lantern. He jerked his head toward an opening in the underbrush. There was a piece of bare ground between two especially large oak trees. These two trees were taller than the other trees in the marsh. They sort of towered over the rest of the marshland. The ground in between the trees was glowing, sort of like sunrise light. Beyond the trees, the marsh was pitch black except for the reflection of the ship's lights on the water. We couldn't see a thing out there and my heart was pounding so hard, I was sure Joe could hear it and tell how scared I was. That was when we heard the sound of Bubba 2 coming through the PALMETTO BUSHES towards the light. He looked at me and Joe, and there was THAT LOOK in his eyes, brighter than I had ever seen, he was telling me that danger was here. That was when the pirate showed himself, right over the light. We almost lost our breath. He had a sword in one hand, and a hook for the other. He glared at me and Joe and we were unable to move. That was when Bubba 2 went to him. He walked toward him real slow. Just then three other pirates began to appear in a transparent way. Bubba 2 was on his haunches and the hair was standing right up straight on his neck and his back, all the way to the tip of his tail. He smelled evil, BIG TIME!

That's the only time I ever saw Bubba 2 growl. It sent the hair bristling up on my neck. I wanted to shout, but I couldn't move, I was frozen. The main pirate growled at us with the most horrible look on his face. He was looking right at me. Then, he disappeared into the air. He just faded away. When he faded, the others just floated upward into the trees. I thought I had swallowed my heart. We suddenly became unfrozen and the three of us ran as fast as we could. We didn't realize how far away we had gone from the oyster roast. When we got to the

camp, we were out of breath. The fishermen were all looking at us. Pa Pa looked at Joe's grandpa, and said, ironically, "These boys look like they've seen a ghost." The party was breaking up. They all shook hands and said good-bye. I couldn't talk all the way home. Pa Pa thought I was asleep. That was fine. I couldn't talk. The lump in my throat was still there the next morning. I never went back into that marsh on Folly Beach. Ever.

Now Joe and me are still best friends. We still go fishing

and crabbing and shrimping together up in Charleston.

But things have been different ever since that night. We

never told anyone what happened. We swore to

secrecy on the graves of the pirates never to tell.

It was a long time before Bubba 2 wanted to wander off alone. He seems to be

more careful than he used to be. Even though Joe and me used to play pirates most

every day, we just don't play that anymore. It seems as though the game might

call back the ghosts and we sure don't want that to happen.

Sometimes in the off-fishing season, Joe and me have time to hunt a little with

Bubba 2. We took up hunting to fill in the time that we used to play pirate. We

mostly hunt for WILD TURKEY and MARSH HENS.

Sometimes we hunt for mallards so Granny can have roast duck

on Sundays. We never really hunt for anything bigger, except once

when we hunted down a coon. That's the kind of

hunting you need a coon dog for, though. Bubba 2 prefers

to take after the winged animals of the water. So usually, we follow the lead of our

hunting dog. Granny really depends on us to bring in some extra special game for

her. Since she never goes into town, it gives her the chance to cook a special Sunday

feast. She is a real good

cook too. One night, we

were having a real treat,

OYSTER STEW and

roast duck—compliments

of Bubba 2.

During supper, Granny looked right at me and she said something that took my

appetite away. She asked me and Joe if we had ever seen a strange light out in the

swamp when we were out hunting in the evenings with Bubba 2. Well, I excused

myself from the table,
and I think that was the
worst I felt since
Halloween night. I guess
Granny knew something
by the look on my face.

Granny had old ways and she could see through me like a glass of water. That was

the last time she ever asked. I guess she knew. So if you ever go out into the marsh

at night on Halloween, remember me and Joe and Bubba 2. The Lowcountry is full
of old souls. I guess some of them you can see and some of them you can't.

THE END

GLOSSARY TERMS
AND LOWCOUNTRY CRITTERS

ANDIRONS: A pair of iron stands used to support wood burned in an open hearth.

BARRIER ISLANDS: Sandy isles running parallel to the Atlantic and Gulf coasts. They protect the mainland from the effects of sea storms. It is estimated that there are 295 major barrier islands along the coastal states from Maine to Texas. The terrain is characterized by a beach system with offshore bars, surf and shifting beach, grassy dunes, and interior wetlands.

BATEAU: Handmade flat bottom boats that are used for harvesting oysters.

BELTED KINGFISHER: Big-headed, double crested lagoon bird. Lives on diet of frogs, beetles, and lizards.

BLUE CRABS: Crustaceans that are blue in color and are used as a staple along the coast.

BOAT TAILED GRACKLE: A black bird with keel-shaped tail, diet consisting of snails, crabs, grasshoppers, and palm berries.

BOB WHITE: A black quail with white throat that stays camouflaged in pine slash and briar patches.

BROWN PELICAN: The largest sea bird. Measures 4-feet long with a 7-foot wingspan. The stretchy pouch holds and drains 6-8 quarts of water after a dive.

CAST NETS: Fishing nets that are designed to catch sea life by the swing of the net into the water, then pulling up the harvest by hand onto the shore or boat.

CATTLE EGRET: Eats insects in herds of cattle. It is the only wading bird that feeds upon land. Immigrated to the Lowcountry riding trade winds by way of Europe, Asia, and South America.

COASTAL BREEZES: These are onshore and offshore breezes that make life more pleasant along the coastline and barrier islands.

COLLARD GREENS: A green leafy plant resembling spinach that is cooked and eaten with pork and corn bread.

DOLPHINS: Bottle-nosed dolphins are marine mammals that thrive in abundance along the coast of the Lowcountry.

DOUBLE CRESTED CORMORANT: Diving birds with 52-inch wingspans. They spread wings half open to dry in the breeze.

FIDDLER CRAB: A small crab, one of whose claws is disproportionately large.

FISH CROW: A shore bird that will also dive down 20 feet to schooling fish. Eats grasshoppers, nest eggs and clams.

FLATLANDS: The marshy land along the coast of barrier islands and along the coast of the Lowcountry.

FOLK TALES: Stories that are passed along by word of mouth from one generation to the next.

FROGMORE STEW: A Lowcountry stew made of shrimp, sausage, onions, and corn on the cob.

GRABS: Large metal tongs used to harvest oysters from the beds along the shoreline.

GULLAH TALES- Folk tales of the Lowcountry.

GULLS: There are four types of gulls: Herring gull, Ring-billed gull, Laughing gull, and the Bonaparte's gull. Their diet consists mainly of fish, rodents, grasshoppers, and trash.

HOECAKES: A cake that is made of cornbread batter, and fried in pork fat. During plantation times this cake was cooked over an open fire in the fields, with field hands using a hoe as a skittle, thus the name.

LIVE OAK TREES: Large deciduous trees of the Southeastern United States, usually growing around the coastal areas.

LOWCOUNTRY: The coast of South Carolina from above Charleston stretching downward to the coast of Savannah.

LOWCOUNTRY MAMMALS: Possum, mole, bottle-nosed dolphin, gray fox, Carolina cougar, bobcats, gray squirrel, raccoon, bat, cotton rat, marsh rabbit, wild boar, white tailed deer, marsh tackys, shrew, river otter.

LOWCOUNTRY REPTILES AND AMPHIBIANS: Lagoon turtles, copperhead, cottonmouth, Eastern diamondback rattler, timber rattler, rat snake, loggerhead sea turtle, and chameleon.

LOWCOUNTRY SHORELIFE: Hermit crab, oyster, sand dollar, sea star, clams, and fiddler crab.

MARSH: A low wet land, a swamp.

MENHADEN: A marine fish of the Eastern United States used in making fertilizer.

NAVIGATE: To travel by water, to sail over or on.

OCEAN WINDS: Northeasters are trade winds that accompany cold fronts with wind velocities to 25 miles per hour, which often blow for 48 hours or more.

OYSTER ROAST: A gathering for the purpose of cooking oysters slowly over a steaming fire.

PALMETTO BUSHES: Semi-tropical fan like bushes that live in the underbrush of the sandy and swampy areas.

PIED BILLED GREBE: Migrating birds who nest in floating rafts of rotting grass.

SANDPIPER: A wading bird living at the water's edge. Their diet consists of fiddler crabs, crustaceans, insects, and eggs. Most sandpipers are small and spotty.

PLANKTON: These microscopic animals live in the sea currents, or in the ocean layers, and are a staple food of the sea.

PLOVERS: Coastal birds that seldom wade, but stay between wet sand and high tide-swash. They live on a diet of insects, sand hoppers, and hermit crabs.

QUILT: A warm, padded bed cover usually handmade from remnants of cloth.

RED TAILED HAWK: This bird has a 4 1/2-foot wingspan. It scours the countryside for mice, rats, rabbits, squirrels, and snakes.

SEA WATER: Water that flows from rivers and streams channeled into the oceans. As the mainlands drain, salts from rocks and soil float with rainwater into the sea. Evaporation removes the fresh water, but leaves the heavier salts behind.

SHRIMPING: Trolling the ocean with shrimp-sized nets to insure the primary catch of shrimp. Shrimping has a specific season and fishermen troll by the height of the tide in each 24-hour period.

SHUCKING: The art of removing oysters from their shells.

SINGLES: Oysters that are detached from clusters.

SNOWY EGRET: A large wading bird with pure white plumage. Each has 50 curving plumes which fluff up with a breeze or movement.

SPANISH MOSS: A silvery gray plant that lives on the live oak trees of the Lowcountry, giving them an ethereal look.

TERN: Close in kin to gulls. There are four main types of terns: Caspian tern, Royal tern, Least tern, and Foster's tern. They dive into the surf for a main diet of fish and shrimp.

TIDAL CURRENTS: These waves occur when the incoming or outgoing mass of water increases in height and forward motion along the coast. Rollers and breakers may occur from wind action on the open ocean. Swells and ridges move across the ocean taking many shapes and sizes. The period is the height and distance between waves.

TURKEY VULTURE: A scavenger of carrion. They have 6-foot wings and a sharp hook on their beak.

UNDERTOW: A powerful current below the surface which flows back to the sea from the beach. The most powerful undertow is caused by the steepest shoreface.

WILD TURKEY: A large bird measuring 4 feet and weighing 20 pounds. Their diet consists mainly of acorns, hickory nuts, insects, poison ivy, fruits, and grass seed.

WOOD IBIS: Four foot high white bird with a buzzard-like black neck and head. Wings span 5 1/2 feet. Diet consists of crayfish, snakes, and fish.

AFTERWORD

LOWCOUNTRY HISTORY

The coast of the South Carolina Lowcountry has been a haven for ships since the 16th century. In the creeks and rivers which are deep enough, shrimp boats float at low tide. Wharves are outfitted to receive the catch brought in by the fishermen. These docks provide mooring and electricity. They provide fresh water for the next trip. In the winter, boats are refurbished before the shrimping season starts. All major repairs are done before the season begins. Decks need to be replaced. Wood often needs to be restored. The effort to keep equipment in working order takes the constant energy of the fishermen. Shrimp boats must be periodically hauled to shore for cleaning and refitting. RAILWAYS are specially built boat repair yards where big boats can be hauled out of the water. The corrosive salt and sand make it necessary to constantly repair commercial boats. Fishing nets must be mended daily as they are being used.

In the Lowcountry, animal power has been replaced by tractors and trucks. Oxen, mules, and horses have mostly disappeared. One exception is the MARSH TACKY, a special breed of horse still used to till gardens and small fields. The horses symbolize the spirit of the Lowcountry.

The local diet changes seasonally with the vegetables in the garden. Hunting for game determines the menu. Sugar cane is grown in the family garden. The sugar cane is cut and taken to a cane mill. The owner of the mill sometimes takes part of the syrup in exchange for payment.

Shells from oysters and clams are still used for building walls, houses, barns, and roadways as they have been for over a thousand years.